EARWIG COUNTRY

Angela Topping was born in Widnes to working-class parents, and now lives in Cheshire. She was educated in Liverpool for over a decade, gaining two Literature degrees at the University. She also gained an M.Ed. from Chester University. She is a wife, mother and grandmother.

She is the author of nine collections of poetry. Her poems have appeared in over a hundred anthologies, and in journals including *Poetry Review*, *The North*, *Magma*, *Stand* and *The Dark Horse*. Her pamphlet *Hearth* was a Poetry Book Society Pamphlet Choice in 2015. She is a former Writer in Residence at Gladstone's Library.

ANGELA TOPPING
Earwig Country

Valley Press

First published in 2024 by Valley Press
Woodend, The Crescent, Scarborough, UK, YO11 2PW
www.valleypressuk.com

ISBN 978-1-915606-22-8
Cat. no. VP0224

Copyright © Angela Topping 2024

The right of Angela Topping to be identified as the
author of this work has been asserted in accordance with
the Copyright, Designs and Patents Act 1988.

All rights reserved. No part of this publication may be
reproduced, stored in or introduced into a retrieval system,
or transmitted in any form, by any means (electronic,
mechanical, photocopying, recording or otherwise) without
prior written permission from the rights holders.

Cover and text design by Jamie McGarry.
Cover photograph by Judy Dean.

Printed and bound in Great Britain by
Imprint Digital, Upton Pyne, Exeter.

Contents

The Word 11

I. COMING OF AGE

Mother of Pearl 15
Sometime Before Myra 16
Miss Mulroy 17
Biscuit Barrel 18
My Sister Poses as a Beatnik 19
The Collecting Dolls 20
Coffee in Calvert's 21
Summer School Skivvy 22
Oxford Covered Market 23
Etchings 24
Fiat Lux 25
Missing the Point 27
Woolly Back 29

II. LOVE POEMS

Love Chronicles 33
Safety Instructions 34
Boot Sale Find 35
One Week Married 36
Big Umbrella 37
Light and Moths 38
The February House 39
The Beekeeper 40
With This Ring 41

III. FORAGING

Foraging 45
Earwig Country 46
Mermaid's Tears 47

Seaham Sea Glass in Winter 48
Green Glass Vases 49

IV. NATURE IN TROUBLE

Salgados Wetlands 53
Magnolia 54
The Valley Where Willows Grow 55
The Great Snowdrop Orchestra 56
Painting Snow 57
Starlingcide 58
Parley 59
Honest John 60
Summer Hedgerow 61
Fern 62
The Last Queen 63

V. MENTAL HEALTH

The Riddle of Angela 67
The What Ifs 68
Stone Dress 69
Stress 70
Ballad of the Lost Girls 71
Patching the Cashmere 72

VI. THE BODY

What the Body Knows 75
Portrait Photographer 76
Waking 77
Writing in the Body 78
Beneath the Skin 81
Steps 82
Scent Bottles 83
Hospital Chairs 84

VII. FAMILY

Plank Figurine 87
Marianne at the Window 88
Missing Marianne 89
Not My Daughter 90
Tracing the Family Face 92
Returning to Castle Museum, York 93
The Britannia Ring 94
Dear Dad 95
Folding Scissors 96

VIII. MOURNING

Bereavement 99
A Drink of Water 100
Registering the Death of Anthony 101
Deferment 102
Close 103
While You Go on Mourning 104
Another May 105
Each One of Us Alive 106
In Waterstone's Café, Liverpool 107

IX. WOMEN IN LIFE AND LITERATURE

Miranda Plans 111
Writing Broken-Hearted 112
Maggie Tulliver Saved 113
Nita's Knitted Wardrobe 114
Cheshire Dig 2529 116

Acknowledgements 118

*In the theatre, there is always that desire
not to break the silence following a great performance
even with applause;*
                  *the same sometimes with music
when you're so attentive you become 'the music
while the music lasts.'*

    from 'Once at Lumb Bank', from Matt Simpson's final collection *In Deep* (Shoestring Press, 2006)

The Word

In the beginning, there was only one word.

Pointing helped, but it was hard to differentiate
between godwater, godapple, godtree,
godhome, godfood, godlove.
People soon needed a word for NO.

So they went native, rebelled, invented.
Words were catching, flew about like birds,
migrated. Soon they were everywhere.

God didn't approve. It wasn't right.
The word was his word. So he had a think.
The idea, when it came, was brilliant.

I'll give them words, he said, *too many*.
He chopped up their common language
into hundreds, each with its own words.

That'll teach them, he said.

I. COMING OF AGE

*Where do they go, those things of little consequence
we don't recall discarding?*

Mother of Pearl

See how the button's outward face
plays with light as I turn it, iridescent
as silk is. A slowly opening eye,
edges easy on the fingertips.

Turn it over. The shank is cracked
where the hole was bored, marred
by a sliver of red, like a thread of jam.
Layers of pearl are chipped away.

Ringed like the inside of trees:
the marks of the machine that made it.
My mother prized such buttons,
threaded them together

a strange bracelet to fit a baby wrist.
She labelled them 'real pearl buttons'
in her schoolgirl-neat blue biro.
Such are the small parts of her I still have.

Buttons from her blouses, fastened
by her quick fingers as she dressed,
where I rested my dark small head
lullabied by the rise and fall of breath.

Sometime Before Myra

Even now I wonder, was I right about him,
the man who asked us if we'd like to see his rabbits?
I'd heard whispers of kids being *interfered with*.

I was wrapped in a scarf of mother's fears,
with spells knitted tight against the dark,
and pinned to my vest was the holy scapular.

'Don't go with him! Run for the fair!'
Although *my mother said I never should
go with the gypsies,* it was only a rhyme.

We ran across the road to brassy lights:
the Wurlitzer, bobbing ducks, pink candy floss,
past the gun range, looking for a stranger to trust.

Men had *urges*, couldn't help themselves
our mums said. A woman could never hurt us,
though we should never get into anyone's car.

The dodgem woman hurried us to church.
She rang the priest's bell, gabbled our story.
Our mothers cried when they came to collect us.

Walking home past waste-ground newly fenced
where he said his rabbits lived, I'd see,
through wire mesh, an orange plastic ball.

Miss Mulroy

When my writing is less than perfect,
elegance overtaken by speed, she frowns
at the marred paper, tuts without sound.
The shadow of a ringed finger
points to the blot I've made.

A crisply typed page pleases her.
A thing worth doing is worth doing well.
Sometimes I find a book's been disturbed,
left open at a page I'm meant to recall:

a poem learned by heart, a story
shared long ago, when I was her favourite
and she my saviour, strict but fair,
judging, demanding *good better best.*

I still have the gift she gave me,
engraved with my name, a parting glass.
If I try, I can hear her breathe on it,
the rasp of silk as she polishes it clean.

Biscuit Barrel

It wasn't used for keeping biscuits in –
but held the sediment of the living:
missing buttons, coins no longer legal tender,
marbles, nuts, every kind of broken bit
that might one day be needed. First place
to rummage, its tipped out contents
sagged skirts between thighs, or rolled
off spread-out newspaper.

Metal handle, lid curled like piecrust –
we'd sometimes Brasso although it wasn't brass.
Cream-cracked china stuff with flowers on
in blues and pinks and greens, a blowsy bunch.
My fingers enjoyed the smooth cool weight
of ball bearings, the squashiness of washers,
as I rooted for bits to make necklaces
idly sifting those forgotten, unsorted things.

Last time I remember seeing it was on a sideboard
in my parents' house, still holding its bellyful of junk.
Were it to be offered now, I would refuse
but long to once more run my fingertips
around its curious lid, rattle the contents.
Where do they go, those things of little consequence
we don't recall discarding?

My Sister Poses as a Beatnik

That summer, my sister chopped her hair,
swapped ponytail for bob
exchanged dirndl flounces for slacks and sweater.

The photo fooled her boyfriend into asking
Who's the hot chick? He drove a Cortina,
ice blue, pale as summer skies.

I was still a tomboy, playing outside
endless days on my trike, or running wild,
dress tucked in knickers, skinned knees.

My sandals skirted rubble, as I picked dandelions
on waste ground left from bombed-out houses,
hands stained from muck and Jubbly drip.

For a moment, I envied her sophistication,
but then turned back to dolls and books,
shaking my head over the shallowness of men.

She smoked cigarettes with a long holder,
wore pearls, spoiled her white leather handbag
indenting a CND logo in blue biro.

I carried on being twelve years younger,
that gap between yawning ever wider.
Now I see my future in her face.

The Collecting Dolls

The sisterhood of six-inch dolls,
lined up in national dress,
an endless Miss World pageant,
stuffed themselves into my box bedroom:

extravagant Miss Spain all ready to flamenco
in frills and pinned bun, glued castanets;
Miss India, pretty in pink sari and bindi;
a Manx doll my dad encouraged me to buy.

Best of all, the Native American dolls
with real leather dresses, cute papooses,
beads and quiverfuls of arrows.
I loved to stroke the calfskin of their skirts.

These are the few among the many,
intaglio or painted eyes, legs standing
to attention like a rainbow guard,
all those eyes watching over me.

Most were packed off to the loft,
remained, stifled in a suitcase,
when the house was sold, their little
plastic hands beating a tattoo on the lid,
trying to get out, reclaim their passports.

Coffee in Calvert's

The shop thought itself above most people.
How we dared go in I'll never know:
small town department store, where time
was bottled, and glass cases sat in judgement.

Just into our teens, we learned to sew
narrow velvet ribbon into headbands
and week on week go back for more.
Then comes the time we climb the stairs

go up into the cafe, where even our mothers
never venture. Trying to work out how
to order milky coffee from the starchy waitress,
trickier than Latin homework.

Other customers tote stiff paper bags
with new hats, tissue-wrapped cashmere jumpers,
stain china rims with Max Factor colours.
We pay no heed to their narrowed eyes.

We are learning to sip like young ladies,
to dab at foam moustaches, biting back giggles
as we count out our brass on hot palms,
proud of haberdashery thrift.

Summer School Skivvy

Books, pencils, even stones, crashed in
through the high window of the practice room,
stung my hands as I grappled with Chopin.
They'd giggle and run away, their footsteps
pattering though polished corridors.
Where are they now, those girls
who shattered my afternoon solace?

No one mentioned it, not a flicker,
though they commented *Don't you sweep well?*
I skivvied while they skived.
They were destined for higher things,
but chose to spend summer pretending work
at boarding school, not home with distant parents,
no local friends to bitch with.

I stuck it out a week, then handed in my notice.
*I've never heard of anyone being prejudiced
against southerners,* headmistress said.
I told her these precious little madams
had hounded, belittled and excluded me.
Her eyes went wide when I told her she,
in all her tweedy arrogance, had let it happen.
Why don't you teach them some manners?
I hope I said, before leaving to catch my train
back Up North to A levels, university,
my hard-won future, while she gaped after me.

Oxford Covered Market

Whiff of haddock, rank as Widnes fishmongers,
the sea gone bad in gutters of scales and blood.
Heavy scent of wax and herbs, as sole
swim past blueberry and vanilla candles.

Somewhere, Mum, you and I could have
wandered in, across cobbles, past tubs
of bunched flowers, you purposeful
like me today, with errands to perform,
bargains to hunt out.

Remember that auction stall where women
would scream out bids and I'd be bored?
Today's prices would appal you,
who once bought me a satin blouse
for twelve and six, to jaunty at the theatre.

What would you have said to see me
fork out for Italian leather shoes?
Oxford Market's quaint but sanitised,
a life away from Widnes Market
and Albert's Walk Round Store.

Etchings

Answer a cliché with a cliché. Last train home,
me at 17 and a man, persuading.
*Get off at my stop, come back to my place,
see my etchings.* Schoolgirls like me
didn't go near men like him, so much older,
only one thing on his mind.

His feet on the seat cutting off the exit
showed me he meant every word.
Had I refused he could have done
anything to me, right there in the carriage,
thrown my raped body out onto the track
when he'd finished with it.

I answered his etchings with my own artifice:
a boyfriend so jealous he would kill him
for even speaking to me. Six foot six,
a Widnes prop-forward, meeting me
at the station, would come and look for me
if I didn't get off safely.

Half an hour on a screaming diesel to hell
talking fast to save my life, my stop,
another man getting off at another door.
He must have heard it all but kept silent,
asked me if I was okay. Too little, too late.
I am now! I threw at him.

And there on the station was my truth,
my dad, solid as wood, ready to strangle
a dragon for me, though old and infirm.
My dad, who'd taught me my worth,
come a tired mile to walk me home.
The last last train I ever caught alone.

Fiat Lux

for Mark

I went looking for you –
my university best friend:
across complex circuitry like those
subtle connections we always had
from the moment I picked you up
in that awful Johnson lecture.
Afterwards we went for beers,
cheese butties, in the Augustus John.

You were the friend
I'd come to uni to meet,
someone to talk books with
who wouldn't think me strange.
I'd thought there'd be more
than just two of us.

You and I
would analyse Western art
on a twenty minute bus ride,
chew over lectures, swap ideas
about poetry, philosophy, ancient times.

You with your connie-onnie Scouse
and suspicious scowl,
so shy you'd not spoken to a soul
till I bounced up in third year,
gave you no choice. Did you
never understand that talking to you, I felt
part of the world I yearned to join?

All these years later, I ring your parents,
their old number found in an address book
I'm throwing out. They'd moved,
but Speke being Speke, someone knew them.

So I find myself speaking to you,
for the first time since we finished postgrad
in 77. You're okay, about to go working abroad.

No point keeping in touch.
Perhaps you're right. Perhaps it's enough
that mediaeval angels swarmed
over Liver Building skies, and we were
drunk on literature, minds like light bulbs;
those heady two years when we were friends,
still young and full of words.

Missing the Point

My tutor in American Studies
punished me with a B+
for showing excessive enthusiasm
for Emily Dickinson.

Told her, I'd come to university
to enjoy myself. Oh, parties,
drinking, nightclubs?
Nope, reading and lectures.

All I'd ever wanted –
the freedom of vast libraries,
excited conversations about books,
finding new authors to love.

I showed her my poem.
about my friend Celia
who'd come from Trinidad
to Liverpool on her own,

half a world away
to *The Blind School*
for A levels and degree.
The tutor whose name I forget

rewrote my poem to show me.
Hers was about an old man
tapping across concrete
with his white stick.

That wasn't my Celia
who was always laughing
who'd take your arm
as a good friend, pass unnoticed,

ask me if two shades
of red were a good match.
When I think of her, I think
of bright turquoises, oranges.

No white man with white stick
tapping his disability on concrete
could replace my Celia.
No one ever could.

'The Blind School' refers to the Royal School for the Blind, Liverpool.

Woolly Back

Long before Superlambananas,
there were woolly backs like me.
What does it take to belong to a city?

Mum pulled me up Brownlow Hill
where God himself dwelled in cathedral crypt
to bring another bag of milk bottle tops.

In Lewis's crèche I chopsticked for hours
on a white baby grand, while Mum
scurried round rainy streets for Christmas gifts.

West Derby's sandstone walls enclosed
my grammar school years, when Widnes girls
turned bullies and Scousers were my friends.

167 Finch Lane's cocoa and flannelette sheets
cocooned me on nights the Crosvilles
made their slow progress home too late.

Fell in love with theatre there, wearing
jumble sale cocktail dresses to the Playhouse,
preferred the Everyman's edginess.

Lugged books from the English section
to the dome of Picton Library
to write notes from halfway up to heaven.

All honoured and degreed, in cap and gown,
Mum and Dad awkward at drinks receptions,
I woke from the dreamtime of university.

Liverpool stamped its dark tattoos on me
in traces of language, the company I keep
but still it pushes me away. I cannot claim it.

II. LOVE POEMS

Love, lift me up on dusky wings

Love Chronicles

Two young ones listening to records
while they held each other
or fought shy, in the early days.
Latin prose neglected on the bureau,
parents making Sunday tea below.

The record was tipped from its sleeve
white paper inner removed,
supported by spread fingertips
on the underside of the label, the edge
resting in the crook of the thumb.

'Spiral Staircases' or 'Love Chronicles'
gently lowered onto turntable,
needle's arm weighted with sixpence,
tenderly swung, placed with precision,
on the already rotating disc.

From the already rotating disc,
tenderly swung, placed with precision,
needle's arm weighted with sixpence,
gently lifted 'Let me down Easy'
and 'Cindy's Crying'

resting in the crook of her thumb,
the edge supported by spread fingertips
on the underside of the label,
white paper inner replaced,
the record slid back into its sleeve.

Parents making Sunday tea below,
Latin prose neglected on the bureau.
They no longer hold each other
or fight shy, in these latter days,
after 'The Dangling Conversation'
one young one listening to records.

Safety Instructions

Use email to aim
wait until you are alone
before replying.
Do not agree to meet.

Do not believe a word.
Take everything to mean
the exact opposite
but realise

one sentence in ten
will be true
and will punch you
in the gut.

Communicate through song
or any other code.
Take rage to mean love,
silence as missing you.

Harbour no regrets
not even on Sundays.
Take a kilner jar
seal up memories

bury it in the darkest
corner of the garden.
Do not mark the spot
with an X.

Boot Sale Find

New Selected Poems 1966-1987, Seamus Heaney,
Faber and Faber 1990

Oh Sarah, did no one ever tell you:
you can't win a teenage boy's love
by giving him an altered poetry book
even when it's by Seamus Heaney

whose brogue is soft as butter.
Your drawings of a couple embracing,
your blue-biroed poems, fastened in
with innocent blobs of blu-tack,

your coy underlinings in pencil –
those aren't going to impress.
Teenage boys want to be let into
the secret of your shy nipples.

They want their hands in your pants,
not *All my love* messages in books
their mums might find, quiz them about.
I've been there too, know how you feel.

A boy I liked wasn't impressed
when I serenaded him with *Drink to me only
with thine eyes and I will pledge with mine*
on the bus in front of all his mates.

Ben Jonson and Heaney, tender poets both,
don't cut it with his type. I hope you find
a lad who likes you back, not like this one
who sold me your gift for twenty pence.

One Week Married

You lean on the secondhand table
writing thank you notes, still bridal
in white lawn Laura Ashley blouse,
pearl buttons rising to your neck.
Pink garden roses release fragrance
as they gently open in the blue vase.

You're all ready to play *house*.
Kitchen so small you can do all you need
from the sink. There will be times
there's no food in the cupboard for tea.
But you don't care. You hang washing
under the car-port, grow vegetables.

No one can tell you how it will be,
the flaws and stains which will blot
your future. Believe me, you don't
want to know the sorrows to come.
Ride them out one by one. In forty years
you will still be here, writing.

Big Umbrella

A shared umbrella
makes a patter house
a pavilion for lovers
or closest friends

a private world
secret society
when summer rain
is a kiss-bringer

it takes balance
tacit agreement
linked arms to keep
two people dry.

Light and Moths

Moths are dazzled by the light,
spiral towards it, maddened,
not so much attracted as yanked,
hypnotised but hating the blindness,
lose their way, dragged into the vortex.

Love, lift me up on dusky wings,
bear me safely from the light.
Dark is a coverlet, warm and close.
You can see through it if you know
where and how to look, with fingertips.

The February House

Winter's gone on too long; we are sick of it.
The cold grips the garden, sealed off
by damp and frost and ice.

What's to look forward to, when spring's
another place far from here? But when
sun breaks out through flat cloud

weak but present, and snowdrops push up
their green finger shoots, there's our first
child to celebrate, coming this month.

Snow can still fall in February, caking
every daffodil with powder, covering lawn,
enough for a first snowman.

The fire is heaped with coal. Little tickling flames
rise up behind the glass door, and the coming child
a lit candle in our window.

The Beekeeper

He can lose himself in his bees
tending to their dark mysterious needs.
Who knows what he does out there
in his bee shed, wearing his white suit
with its netted hood.

He brings honey and nubs of beeswax,
the only signs of secret labours.
They are his golden gifts,
while in the garden white beehives hum
heady with their secrets.

With This Ring

My wedding band
impossible to ease off
fleshy ring finger
embedded over forty years
of a changing body.
Even on dull days
it gleams, reflects light
untarnishable.
I will wear it till I die.

My ring finger is naked
it wears only the mark
of the wedding ring
I had cut off;
its gold band sliced
severed from my hand
like a broken promise.
Just a symbol, no more.
Even the sign of it is enough.

III. FORAGING

Beautiful things have inner horrors

Foraging

Yes to mushrooms, blackberries, nettles for pop,
elderflowers and elderberries, rose hips for syrup.
Wild garlic or ramson for salads and soups.
Never enough wild strawberries to bring home
so pick and cram into mouth, sticky with summer.
Nature sets out a larder for her creatures.

Pebbles and shells from sea margins, bird bones
and feathers, animal skulls – these suit windowsills.
Then vases of pussy-willow, bluebells, ragwort,
even prickled gorse. From country walks
marigold and celandine span the year, cheer
a kitchen table with haphazard sprays of colour.

But sometimes, let your basket stay empty, light as air.
Take nothing but memories, dug up from wild places,
earthy nuggets like truffles: tiddlers fished and replaced
in childhood ponds; that time by the river bridge
you saw a grass snake, blackberrying with your dad.
Leave darker ones in the undergrowth to rot.

Earwig Country

The flowers are white cups, poised upright,
as if waiting to be filled. Bindweed stems
hold them up to the light, like fine porcelain.

I investigated them for scent. A flower like that
must be an olfactory delight, but deep within
dark brown clawed things crawled.

As children we believed earwigs aimed
to enter our heads through the portal
of our ears, bury themselves in our brains.

Beautiful things have inner horrors
I learned to be wary of. The hedges held aloft
whole tea services of bone china, pure white

full of the plotting of earwigs. Put your ear
too close and you will hear them, whispering
in their marble citadels. They are coming for us still.

Mermaid's Tears

The sea had no choice but to accept
this glass jetsam: industrial waste, thrown in
at day's end. Nor to winkle it out
from forgotten wrecks, nor slurp from rivers
decanting themselves into the deep.

Fragments swirled in its dark salt,
smashed, ground down
as over decades the sea roughed them
then threw them onto beaches
with its bellyful of pebbles.

These icy shreds of light
become tongues of flame, sun-licked.
With the next tide the sea
claims them back, brings fresh pieces.
Gather these chips of colour when you can.

Frosted like sweets dipped in sugar,
pitted, varicoloured: aqua, white, dark green
easy to find. Cobalt blue, red, grey, lavender
rarer gems. Each shape is unique,
some flat, others rounded chunks.

Sort into colours, hoard in jars,
stroke their silken surfaces.
Visualise every beach where the sea
flung them at your feet, how they looked
the moment they caught the light.

Seaham Sea Glass in Winter

The sea dashes and rolls
while we play catch with it
stepping into its trail of foam
as bubbles dissolve and break.

We pick through fresh pebbles
for fragments of glass, sea-scratched
smoothed into these nubs,
half jewel, half solidified drops.

Worth the punishing steps
freezing wind and rain
to find these chips of light
some clear, some pale green,

some lapis blue, or jade.
How long before the sea
pounds them to powder
with its relentless churning?

Green Glass Vases

Vaseline uranium: a pair but *she* has them both,
Mum wanted each of her girls to have one.
My sister wouldn't hear of splitting them.

I was dumb to answer back, tongue bitten,
eyes clouded, still seeing Mum wrapped
in bloody sheets, then lily pale on hospital cot,

not hankering after what was in the china cabinet,
silent cupboards or abandoned wardrobe.

She was in command, fingers quick to roll
treasures in newspaper, pack boxes, as if that
could bring back a mother dead too soon.

These vases Mum filled with bluebells,
or whatever flowers I brought back for her
from cycle rides with Dad, my arms never empty.

Thirty years on, Sister sets out only one.
Is mine smashed, wrapped in newspaper
dumped in a bin? Or are they still a pair?

Mum would have been cross about it. But somehow
no one tells my sister she can't have what she wants.

IV. NATURE IN TROUBLE

Enclosures still sweep across our woods and fields

Salgados Wetlands

We've puzzled over maps to travel here,
arrive to a hotel complex moored in the wetlands –
a cruise ship rooted into earth, locked in a bottle.

Can't find our way to the bird reserves for this brown hulk
squatting in scrubland, with boardwalks to the beach,
balconies stacked like cardboard shelves, palm trees

keeping its secrets, every gate except one locked
against short-cut seekers. We walk through car parks,
past security fences, in relentless heat

while, like the tick of a bomb about to detonate,
cicadas keep up their crick-crick lament. The hotel
is silent, a film set for some post-apocalyptic drama.

I wear my nowhere-is-too-posh-for-me face
as we stop for sandwich and coffee in a pool bar,
the only part open to the public.

Beyond the fish tank of doomed lobster,
the toilets are all limestone and marble.
I snoop through forests of parasols to blue water.

The wetlands were worth our walk. Green water
is rich with turtles we lean on the bridge wall
to photograph. The lake's shores show us

spoonbills and avocets. Grebe ruffle the surface.
I wonder whether hotel vacationers come here
on their blank days, remark that the birds

are not as pink as they are in zoos, while
off in unreachable distance, going about their business,
a flock of flamingos congregates to fish.

Magnolia

This is no bland neutral to pacify a sitting room.
Magnanimous, the buds shed their light,
standing like candles on dark branches.

No two flowers are alike.
Each centre a deep pink blush,
stretching threads down the petal's length

to the expensive edge of its page.
When they slowly open, the intimate heart
is revealed in all its purity

until each one lets its petals go,
gives itself up to the unsubtle summer,
makes a constellation on the cobbled yard.

The Valley Where Willows Grow

*The above is a view which will never
be seen again by mortal eye*
Caption to a sketch of the valley, 1840

Hostelling in the 1970s, I would gaze
past *Keep out* signs at Thirlmere,
its waters free of boats and swimmers
that busied the length of Windermere.
Striding Edge cut clouds, so I chose softer slopes
to see the mere snaking up the valley,
rippled reflections of dark, close trees
and skies changing from blue to grey.

It captivated me, even before I knew
Wythburn and Armboth lay underneath,
abandoned as the waters rose;
a Celtic bridge straddled wetlands between
Brackmere and Leathes Water. Ruskin wrote
they should drown Manchester instead
but pure Lakeland water could save lives.
They dammed the valley, planted Canadian
Sitka spruce to keep the banks intact,
built a brick viaduct, using gravity
to traverse the miles, cleanse the city.

Now broadleaved woods are returning:
namesake willow once more takes its place,
as saplings of oak and rowan grow tall.
Red squirrels settle to thrive and breed.
Wildflowers can spread on forest floor.
Ten miles of paths around the lake
fill with birdsong, bee hum, walkers' hellos.

The Great Snowdrop Orchestra

The great snowdrop orchestra
begins its tuning up, in secret
then pushes out strong notes,
sharp and flat at first
but growing to a harmony.
As earth warms, each small group
prepares to play its part.
Soon *Gerard Parker* taps the music stand,
raises his baton. Each tepal is lifted,
alert, ready to enchant.

Lord Monostictus leads the bass section.
His deep notes underpin the melody
as silver-throated *Ophelia* soars above,
her grace notes embroidering the air,
improbably high. The open quavers
of *Magnet* counterpoint, dancing
up and down the scale effortlessly,
the wind's harp. Full-throated,
Lady Beatrix Stanley bubbles her clarinet.

Viridapice manages percussion
from tangly triangle to deep drum.
There is no music like it, the sonatas
and symphonies of snowdrops
played all over the world.
One day, if scientists continue
their important work in this field,
we may even come to hear it.

Painting Snow

for Gordon Tyrrall

Leaving the paper blank is not enough.
Chinese White deadens the picture.
Payne's Grey or watery Winsor Blue
can help with shadows under trees.
But how to depict March snow
caught in the ruffles of the daffodil
or drowning snowdrops until only the green
is left poking up through a new fall?

Dead leaves are not hard to draw
but when they shrivel and curl
under hard frost, and become laced in silver
they defy Yellow Ochre and Burnt Umber.
Snow blasted into the bark of silver birches
is hard to differentiate
from their own glorious specklement.

Snow reinvents a landscape
hiding its blemishes as though
they have been quietly erased in the night.

Starlingcide

The starling's a showman, natty circus master:
iridescent summer garb spangled purple and blue
turns to star-sprinkled midnight for winter,
lemon beak more subtle than blackbird's orange.

> *There's a man on YouTube shooting starlings,*
> *his air rifle deadly, his laughter maniacal.*
> *He slaughters two pecking at nuts on a feeder,*
> *clinging with legs red as strawberry laces.*

Little mimics, they learn new languages to add
to their own clicks and whistles: impressions
of other birds, and human noise, alarms and ringtones.
In big groups they are loud as a hall full of schoolkids.

> *Now starlings are eating maggots and worms*
> *drugged with Prozac and human despair*
> *males no longer want to sing love songs,*
> *to females gone lethargic and dull.*

Come dusk, they gather from miles wide, to meet,
on telephone wires and bridges, then murmurate
into sky dance, a coiling spirograph, ballet of specks
every bird a pixel in their moving images.

> *Starlicide poison can be purchased online*
> *for those who see these birds as pests.*
> *Death comes sly from behind their defences*
> *not hawks nor falcons but human invention.*

Parley

Conjuring owls is dangerous.
They fix me with their complex eyes.
Disdain is beneath them.

They came to the scream
of a rabbit, but it was only you
imitating the noise exactly.

The screaming rabbit may succumb,
I am no prey. My steel spine,
bone corset, is the match of yours.

I answer in my lark's tongue:
all is well, is well, is well.

Honest John

Well, honest John, how fare you now at home?
John Clare

You said you'd never be grammar's slave,
held fast to your dialect, croodled your thin body
close to the fire, reading Shakespeare, though they called you
uneducated, the peasant poet. How they tried to belittle you.
You railed against editors, fought for your words.

Birds are for watching, not specimens for display.
You softly invite me to observe the nightingale,
but say the robin has a sweeter song. You loved
the dung heap and the rooting pigs, roamed the wild moors
and nearby woods, rejoicing in every flower.

You tell them, John, as they come to chop your elm tree down.
Tell them how it sheltered and kept you safe.
They hanged the mouldiwarps from the very trees, and men too.
Your pen scratched on the paper and would not be silent
as enclosures robbed the peasants of their lives.

Now homes are built on greenbelt land, trees axed.
Enclosures still sweep across our woods and fields.
Fences keep out refugees, but this is no land of honey.
The working classes vote for their own destruction
and once again the poor are starved and cold.

Summer Hedgerow

Tangled
stems, stalks and leaves:
haphazard shelter
for any bird, bug or flying creature
to hide.

                      Sun's eye
                      and predator alike
                      excluded now
                      from this close thatched haven
                      home.

Thorn and bramble
keep out
careless interfering hands
until ripening blackberries
tempt.

                      Foxgloves,
                      violets, cow-parsley
                      and buttercups scatter here
                      striping the hedge with colours
                      randomly.

Hot sun
brings out the scent
a green spice of leaves
the contented buzz of insects
happy.

                      Within the hedge
                      little paths zigzag
                      and twist, rising to different levels.
                      Inhabitants descend,
                      ascend

making
their scurrying
journeys in this wooden city
with purpose like workers
to offices.

                      Each hedge
                      has its own way
                      architecture unplanned
                      its own pot-luck of wildflowers
                      its own language.

Fern

Greenfrond, curlywhirly, fiddlehead,
curlytop, frazzlebrain, Chinese ladder,
shade-lover, spray-grower, hart's tongue,
pattern-maker, seedstrip, maidenhair.
You grow everywhere you can,
each narrow frond is a seed packet
in the making. You fountain out
of a sandstone wall, spout near wells
and house corners, anywhere damp
you can catch hold. You are not simple.
You brighten up the darkest corner
with your feathery joyousness.
You need no flower, your leaves
are special enough to make a show.

The Last Queen

My sisters, deep in our cells, are still feeding me.
But I know I will be their last queen.
The succession dies with me.
My workers toil to bring home supplies
but they hum of too few flowers
They suck on litter, drops of sweetness
that ooze from shiny objects left on the ground.
They fly far. Not all return. The air is poisoned.
Our drones sicken and die on the wing.
Some of my sisters have died in their compartments
become dry as ash. Some never grew enough
to take part in our great enterprise.
Not enough honey now to feed us all.
Why must they place their hope in me?
How can I tell them what I know to be true?

V. MENTAL HEALTH

Who never stops worrying the words

The Riddle of Angela

Who watches the hottest oval of the candle flame, then glozes into words
Who sings the coal fire as it flimmers and flickers on the edges of paper
Who sees afternoon sunlight on a brick wall and is uplifted
Who needs black ink to make the strongest marks in the swiftest ways
Who never stops worrying the words till they give up their truths
Who hates raised voices, harsh shouts, temper-striking eyes
Who lives as a child, reaching for gaudy baubles and wanting her mother
Who hears the cello call and the violin soar, rejoices in the breath-vibrating flute
Who wants to draw forth music from every instrument but never practises
Who tries to keep the clock ticking, the doors open, the kitchen light on and the bread rising
Who fears the door slam, the late night hospital ward, the sudden stop of love
Who craves company yet relishes the peace of alone time
Who longs to keep everyone close but knows the best love lets go

The What Ifs

Not like unwrapping a present
someone you love gives for your birthday
knowing it's a surprise you'll enjoy

more like putting your fingers
into the jaws of a black velvet bag
because you have to, don't want to.

Anything could be inside, lying in wait,
to trap you or do harm. You ask yourself
what's the worst can happen?

Sometimes the worst is getting
the wrong train or being late. Sometimes
there are ways to solve the problem.

But when the worst is death
you know you're in trouble.
Nor can you stay home fretting.

You're too young to box yourself up,
disappear into your own armchair,
so ease your hand inside the bag.

Sometimes what's in there
is a lucky green jade turtle,
cool and composed, on a red silk thread.

Run your fingernail along its carved lines,
you can die just as easily
at home without taking risks.

Stone Dress

A difficult dress to wear,
lacking the glamour of silk,
but suited to all weathers.
Her gown of marble
studded with fossils
took a long time to grow.
It makes her feel safe,
an impermeable cave
where no one can touch her.
Her scarf is a stream,
her shoes woven from green nettles.
She ties her hair with brambles;
her rings are thorns.
Stepping out in this array,
despite the effort of each step,
she's newly bold.

Stress

She is not much more than a baby,
not yet sleeping through the night.
She frets her blankets, starts a siren cry:
there is no comforting her.

She grows fast. Sometimes, she helps:
wearing her plastic pinny at the sink.
She builds up coloured blocks
then smashes with a clatter her wobbly towers.

I'd be bored without her but when she's here
her constant demands wear me gruel-thin.
Can't keep up with her; no wonder
playing chase is her favourite game.

Her doll is stuck with pins, grimaces
in its crib, one eye gone, dressed in rags.
I miss her when she's not here, then find her
careering out of the lift at work.

She stands by my desk, flinging pens,
messing up all my papers
then sits underneath it howling.
She folds herself small

fitting into my briefcase,
rides home with me unseen,
then spills herself on my sofa,
curls up in a ball in my midnight sheets.

Ballad of the Lost Girls

Oh where are you my daughters dear?
Where have my babies gone
that they should up and leave me here
all in this place alone?

Once I had two children dear
who played around my feet.
One's hair was golden as the sun,
the other as black as night.

Their little voices piped all day,
their hands brought stems of flowers.
Together we told many tales
to while away the hours.

They played at fairies in the wood
and rode their bikes around.
Their sturdy legs conveyed them far –
I heard not a sound.

I was busy in the kitchen
making the family tea
I was writing in the book room
when they slipped away from me.

Now I sit in darkness drear
and see no face I know.
Why are all these strangers here?
Where did my daughters go?

Patching the Cashmere

A hug of a cashmere hoodie
worn to rag; previous darning
unsuccessful as more holes opened.
Couldn't bear to throw it away.

I'd loved sinking my hands
into the sideways pockets
until they came away in patches,
my fingers pushing on the stitches.

Scraps from older cashmere
now secured with embroidery:
lazy daisy and running stitch
shapes of blossom in bright shades.

Lockdown gave me restless fingers,
time to fix and heal the fray
but now as gaps are opening,
the more essential mending is.

VI. THE BODY

The flora of the gut do not count in botany

What the Body Knows

The body tends to its own healing skill;
it stitches itself back together, unseen.
Bones knit without clacking needles,
by invisible threads, need only to be held still.

The flora of the gut do not count in botany,
their forms not illustrated in nature guides.
Not fauna, though they swim: sea anemones
moving in a dance to the body's own canny.

And the miniscule eggs of ovaries, the squirming
sperm of the ball sack, know their private work,
respond to their steps in the tango, their pearls
set in a silver ring on ultrasound screen

within the womb's salt sea, dividing and growing,
rubbery blue rope anchors another conundrum.
The body knows when to die, closing its programmes
one by one, until at last organs stop their whirring.

Deep within, below our ken, they know
their teamwork roles. Oh what blues, what purples,
what jewel strings of rubies, rounded cabochons,
secret geodes, coils of unvalued gold.

Portrait Photographer

The Hardmans' House, Liverpool

Do not wear powder; it dulls the skin.
A little lipstick serves to moisturise
like the tea we offer you in china cups.

Be calm. The sitting will take an hour.
There is no need to smile. We wait
for that to happen naturally.

Let me find out about you. We will talk.
Become used to the lights, they dazzle
at first, I know. Take pleasure

in your tea; we use the finest leaf.
Thank you. We shall be in touch
when your picture is ready for collection.

Perhaps you might like to consider
our *Gold* portrait, only a guinea extra.
It will make you appear flawless.

Waking

Not the eyes
nor the tongue: its chatter
stopped in gluey mouth.

Not the body, still
knotted in sleep,
hands folded.

The white quilt and pillow
still spread for the voyage,
the sailing of my night

is not yet docked.
The ears wake first.
I hear

the floorboards ache.
Your question tingles.
I struggle

cannot frame an answer
from my dark and
dream-filled sleep.

Writing in the Body

*

Perhaps I am a bird. Let's say a sparrow.
I dive down a chimney or spurt
through a tall open window
circle round Italian galleries
mistaking art for real landscapes.

Or perhaps I am a fish. Let's say a carp.
I allow Danube's waters to love through me,
conscious of little but survival.
I flick my tail fin and feel its power,
as I glitter in my chain mail.

I am a bee entering the tunnel of a foxglove,
burrowing into air turned pink and freckled.
I bathe in seas of lavender, my fur sticky
with pollen, prepare for the coming cold,
the winter clustering.

A bird again, this time a swallow
I fly high across continents
guided by magnetism or some other
dark force I have to follow,
my companions around me.

I am higher than tall towers;
deeper than oceans; lost
in the music of the spheres;
rooted in the secrets of the earth.

*

Rhythm is easy, iambic heartsong
slipsliding of trochees
complicated butter pats of anapests
being slapped into shape by grooved pine boards,
runaway train of dactyls clacking along.
Scansion is the salve for wounds

but melody arises pianissimo, tentative
trying to find the right key, the phrase
that opens up the arc and soars
until each crotchet and quaver finds
where it belongs on the stave
and the cadence
moves on in inevitable flow
to a new beginning.

*

I buy the salted popcorn, bring a blanket
settle down in the best seats
to watch the movie with my inner eye.
Not just sight but a feely, smells and taste.
My mind's eye is a quality cinema.

But most often, the poem comes
like a lover, to whisper in my ear
teasing phrases I can barely catch,
then runs away laughing.

I need all my skills to interpret
the other side of my brain, pin down
the wriggling, tantalising words.

*

A line or phrase from a forgotten draft
can be prized loose and hammered
into a different poem, like a stud
in an old oak door, or a gem
embedded into silver.

It may wander until it finds
a new place to exist, or be lost
like junk in a jumbled drawer.

Memory too. Polish and shine,
add new flourishes, build it up
till it's bright and new.

But beware. Beware of chanting
the same spells too often
else they may lose their magic.

*

Spooled in my nucleus, the combined threads twisted together,
lie the instructions, the form I took, the knots that make me up.
My mum's blue eyes and fine hair, my dad's plump cheeks
and worker's hands, though unlike his, my cuticles are buried.
I went out into the world where they could never venture
to take my present form. They would not know me now.

Poems choose their form. I listen and do not hold them back,
let them be the things they mean to be, though gnarled
and rambling sometimes like old trees, or neat in the small house
of the sonnet, gathering their blankets round them in rhymes.
There's always my fingerprint, my heartbeat, thrumming
behind them, though they travel far from me.

'Not just sight but a feely' is from Brave New World, *a cinema experience which includes all the senses.*

Beneath the Skin

My heart is a mansion
with all its chambers
decorated in red velvet
linked by the satin ribbons
of my veins. My lungs
nourish rare flowers and trees.
My brain is a maze of corridors
embellished with incredible art
and in the back of my eyes,
upside down and fuzzy,
the world is suspended.

Steps

Steps tempt
      the climber to discoveries:
the bell tower
      with its twisting promise of views;
the slippy staircase
      of a short cut offering itself
through a narrow alley
      to emerge part way up a known street;
rough steps cut into a garden
      or dizzy fellside
stained with lichen and moss
      harbouring fireweed, dandelion
a friendly handrail to haul up
      faltering steps of one
who years ago would have run them.
      Steps measure
more than heights or depths,
      they count frailties and years.

Scent Bottles

She hoarded them for their touch of luxury,
among broken necklaces, odd earrings
on her dusty dressing table:
those last precious inches of floral blends,
saved for a best that never came,
thickening and stale, until all they smelt of
was cheap talcum and wasted days.

My scent bottles are for Eternity, Euphoria,
duty free bargains, for as long as they last.
Their shiny promises whisper in my ears
of romance and foreign skies.
Childhood experiments, making fragrance
from crushed petals, lavender, find
fulfilment in Jo Malone's *Red Roses*.

I splashed on *Aqua Manda*, orange spice
that little girls were not made of, and smouldered
like a femme fatale, until motherhood
grounded me with baby lotion, milk, Napisan.
More expensive, the perfumes of the middle years
leave traces in the air I move through.

These bottles of precious ichor: geraniol, civet, musk,
are stoppered like time, evocative, preserved.
Their delicate pinks and blues, their silvered lids,
gleam on the shelf, their endless summer
a valiant illusion, created in laboratories.
I spray them to keep at arm's length
the slippage of days, fumes of smoke, of soil.

Hospital Chairs

are temporary, belong in a stack
at the corner of the ward. You have to
fetch one, replace it afterwards.
Visitors are clutter. Better to stand,
awkwardly shifting on the spot
knowing your place, until the end
of the appointed hour or the patient
slips again into the privacy of sleep.

are not comfortable. Heavy
metal frames and plastic seats
discourage occupancy. Words
leak out slow from numbed minds
once practicalities are done with:
dirty washing exchanged for clean,
fruit dispersed, squash bottles stowed.
Get well cards begin to bend and fall.

Only the ill have a place to be,
starched into bland pastel beds,
crisp as hospital etiquette, small talk.
They do not want to be there, envy you
the healthful air and petty chores
you walk back into, leaving them
floating like grey balloons, claimed
by a routine which counts you out.

VII. FAMILY

Down the years family faces bloom and fade

Plank Figurine

Moon Mama, halo head,
how many cradles have you rocked?
How many lullabies hummed?

Time traveller, grave survivor,
tell us your riddles, your histories.
Who linked arms with you?

Clay enigma, marked with cuts,
your gold earrings missing,
what will you reveal to our touch?

Marianne at the Window

She asks to be lifted. In response
to my questions, her determined digit
shows me trees, houses, mountains,
as she stands on the wide windowsill
on the first floor, planted firm, a flower.
White pigeons rise as she watches, points.
She is learning new words to say, every day.

We relish these snatched moments
with this little enchanter, so like our child
it could be her, born again, taking us back
on a magic carpet of forever grasslands
as she tastes new words: apple, there, hair.
She cannot yet say Grandma, Granddad.

On this last holiday morning
she holds audience on this podium
the whole vista laid out before her,
and, from across the lawns, she is seen,
waved at by other holiday makers.
She grins, waves back, knowing her right
to be adored. The mist is coming down
hiding the mountains, stealing the view.
Later, we wave her goodbye.

Missing Marianne

That spring she turned Rapunzel,
might as well have been holed up
in a tower without stairs. Her golden hair
grew long, was parted, plaited like wheat.

She went feral, pulled off shoes and socks
to go barefoot. On exercise breaks
she ran deep into the forest, scenting bears.
Her legs grew long as she turned four.

She might as well have been asleep
in a faery castle with barricades of roses,
brambles and raspberry canes, hedged
all round with spells and dreams.

We're still seeking the formula
to unlock the curse, bring her back.

If only a kiss would do, we'd give thousands
to feel her small arms around our necks,
hear her bright chatter jingle like gold coins,
her giggles that turn the sky into sparkle.

She's a schoolgirl now, neat in her uniform,
says it's the best day of her life,
but we can't be there to hear her news,
bend to hug her at the school gates.

We can only send our love in a video
keeping it light, but she knows,
yes, she knows things are not right.

Not My Daughter

For K.

You were my first child, though not born of my flesh.
Something leapt in me when I first saw you:
a parcel held up at the hospital nursery window.
I could not wait to hold you in my arms.

Self-appointed as your protector, not-my-daughter,
I watched over you as you slept, pushed you out
in your pram as, on your own hand, you played
'Round and Round the Garden' and giggled.

We'd play word games for hours, our two heads together
as I taught you to recite a Catullus poem in Latin,
was scolded for painting your toenails pink.
But they took you away from me, not-my-daughter

to live in a high cold house far away. You came back
for visits, your small case packed, heavy with books.
There were times when I could not reach you
as you retreated behind bitter words, teenage and aloof.

We have so many memories, not-my-daughter.
You teaching me Maths to pass an exam;
me making you laugh in the Gallery of Invisible Treasures
my name for empty glass cases in the British Museum.

Your degree day, when, with no tickets booked,
we saw you receive your degree *in absentia*.
Just as well, since you refused to believe that jeans
were disallowed, and anyway, you'd booked no gown.

And if there have been times when you felt
the need to test my love, to see what would survive
I hope you found the answer you required
and know that nothing now can change.

So when you need me in the dark of winter,
to tell me someone you loved has died too young,
you have my number on perfect recall,
my daughter, though not born of my body.

Tracing the Family Face

At first there are no faces, only silhouettes,
grey scale, or pink and blue. Guesswork
patches together scraps from censuses,
half-remembered tales from long ago.

Slowly, studio portraits begin to appear:
one last memento of Daddy going off to war,
wives in Sunday best, on chairs not their own,
children starched to best behaviour.

The rich display out-of-reach oil paintings
in their great houses, but the camera's secret arts
bring to ordinary folk the joy of showing off
how beautiful grandma was at sixteen.

Parents with Box Brownies snap day trips,
wedding scenes, family Christmas, new babies.
Black and white, but hand tinted, fixed up
in passe-partout, framed on the mantelpiece.

At last family resemblances reveal themselves:
older brother wears Mum's Dad's face,
while next brother sports Dad's chubby cheeks
from when he too was 15, becoming a man.

Colour began (like sex, as Larkin tells)
in the 1960s. The family tree lights up,
my eyes the match of Mum's light blue.
Down the years family faces bloom and fade.

Returning to Castle Museum, York

Going there with you, bearing
your slight but clinging weight
as you tried not to slip on cobblestones,
remember? You browsed shop windows,
spilling stories from a head full of memories,
family folklore details I've blurred.

You'd known the world like this:
apothecary jars full of powders,
brass scales, high oak counters to lean on,
where lace was measured and buttons
of glass and pearl counted out for pennies.
You'd dragged on your father's arm
mithering for everything, and getting it,
only child, larded in wintergreen,
wanting aniseed balls and fondant creams.

Our children's feet thunder through,
outrunning the pulling horse whose hooves
are fettered so he can't reach his destination,
impatient for the gift shop, where Dad
might be talked into buying rock, or pencils.
I want to walk through slowly.
There's just a chance you might be here.

The Britannia Ring

Mum's jewel box was purple velvet; where corners frayed
cardboard showed its grey dullness. Flimsy, it barely held
as my child hands rummaged for dressing up props.
The glittering treasures inside were paste or fakes.

Her first wedding ring broke, worn away to sliver, light.
Engagement ring dropped two diamonds, their empty
sockets claws. Were her wedding photo pearls
borrowed for photographs taken weeks afterwards?

In her fifties, she started treating herself to rings
from Liverpool pawn shops, trailing me miles from town.
Weeks before her death, begged me to wear
her dainty Victorian 22 carat pearls and turquoise.

Grown too loose for her, it kept falling into bedsheets.
She liked to see it on my fingers. It no longer fits;
my knuckles now swollen with arthritis. But I keep it still,
in my jewel box, hold back from passing it to daughters.

Dear Dad

It's too long since we saw each other.
In 1978, you went to another country
beyond my reach. I'd like to think
Mum found you there two years later
when she undertook to travel
but I have no faith in the trains.

I'd like to tell you how I still
bake pies the way you showed me;
how I still love flowers, their scents
and country names: celandine,
speedwell and larkspur our litany.
I feel closest to you out of doors.

You smelled of soil and salt, of sweat
and the musk of greenhouse tomatoes.
I don't forget that mark your cigarette left
on the side of the bath; even Ajax
couldn't shift it. I heard you'd given up.

You packed so little for the journey:
that photo of me, your wedding day,
the code you used for love, *I do*,
your children's names, your signet ring.
Thank you for leaving behind
those folding scissors I still use.

I wish you could come back but maps
have been re-drawn, landmarks
obliterated. You wouldn't know me.
But if you get this note, could you send
your recipe for rice pudding? No one
here has a clue how to make it.

Folding Scissors

Father's folding scissors:
for forty years I've cut
my nails remembering him.
Trick scissors, folding
like the moon, to a thin sliver.
Stainless steel, Sheffield made,
sharp as never-blunted grief.

VIII. MOURNING

Just a keepsake to remember her by

Bereavement

How do you come back from this?
asks a friend whose dad just died.
Answer is, you don't. It's more
you have no choice but to survive.

You live on memories. A moment's
forgetting then recalling
again that they have gone forever
though you keep on calling.

A Drink of Water

My mother told me something
she'd never been able to forget:
as a small child, she watched women
keeping company with the dying.
They denied a drink
to the parched lips whispering 'water'.

No, it will only prolong her misery.

Those drops would have let through
another ten minutes of life.
Such power, to cancel death
even for so short a span.

Say you'll give me
water, if I ask for it?

When the time came
she lay in hospital
not at home tended by
hard-faced women whose
business was birth and death
but kindly nurses,
and me by her bedside
offering a sippy cup,
of water she did not want to drink.

Registering the Death of Anthony

Yours wasn't my first death certificate.
Years ago I'd had to register our mum's.
Perhaps I am hardened to it now;
after the anguish, paperwork takes over,
some kind of comfort, a refuge of facts.

I read your list of ailments with interest,
always thought another stroke would kill you.
But no. Ischemic heart disease, like Dad.
So that's what was behind your last email.
Bedtime: getting earlier every night.

Deferment

Grief is a cruel handbag –
its catch snaps shut like jaws.
Inside is buried an old compact,
hankie embroidered with an M
in a huddle of forget-me-nots.
There's a used-up biro, one cherry lipstick,
a purse stained from long-dead hands,
inside only a few pence, a stamp.
The handbag is a stomach
digesting the past. What can be
done with it? It cannot be thrown away.
Best hide it in the bottom of the wardrobe,
an unexploded bomb.

Close

Our neighbour is dying.
Last month his wife died.
Cancer was a guest in their house
far too short a time for him,
too long for her.

We had never been inside their house,
nor they in ours.
The neighbourliness of friendly hellos
difficulties of parking
yappiness of their golden spaniel
decorations on their front door
for birthdays, Christmasses
and all the other fine things
they will not see again –
that was the extent of our relationship.

Lockdown made a piazza
of our turning circle, our neighbour
centre stage with his guitar,
his wife in a headscarf from chemo.
We kept our responsible distance –
Bye Bye Miss American Pie
and *We'll Meet Again*.

We lined the close for her funeral,
now send him messages of cheerfulness.
What else could neighbours do
who never exchanged a hug
nor held him when he wept.

Before the messages arrived
a private ambulance came
while we were all eating dinner,
took our neighbour away
silently to the mortuary.

While You Go on Mourning

Putting words into the mouths of the dead
is too easy; slotting them like old coins
between their frosted lips, so they cannot
spit them back, is too convenient.

He wouldn't have liked that, people say,
about things you want to do.
She wanted me to have this, she claims,
slipping the silver into her bag.

Just a keepsake to remember her by
as a bundle of fivers is pocketed.
They want to help you clear the house:
suddenly treasure trove but still your home.

The dead cannot come back to refute
and so people go on ventriloquising.
If only the dead could return,
shout them all down for a pack of liars

Another May

i.m. Matt Simpson

A leaf, once opened, leads to possibilities;
it's as though you stretched out your hand
to me again. It's May.
Hawthorn blossom froths on hedges.
It's time for you to weed the flower beds,
cut lawns, puffily shoving the mower
up and down the back garden.
Time to set about the pond
so koi can prosper, fill pots
with summer bedding: red geraniums,
the blue scabious you loved so much.
Scented wallflowers stand by the beech hedge
in sunset shades, and the pink roses are in bud.

This month you would have turned 80,
and in some foolish dream of mine
be still standing, talking to neighbours,
while I roll up in the car, come to visit.
You'd throw your arms around me
and we'd go indoors to talk poetry,
books and music. It's seven years, Matt,
since we kept each other going. You had
eighteen years start on me, but now
I'm catching up fast. Only eleven
to go until I match your time alive.
This is my eighteenth elegy for you.

Each One of Us Alive

i.m. Matt Simpson, at Lumb Bank

To have him alive again, vigorous,
his grave cheeks folding to a grin,
the old certainties and uncertainties
resolving to a new book of poetry

is all I could wish for, in these days
where poetry is at my centre.
Even here, he follows me, or do I
follow him? I take his books from the shelf,

recall his poem about Anne Stevenson
reading Elizabeth Bishop aloud here.
His loving ghost whispers
into the silences of places like this.

In Waterstone's Café, Liverpool

i.m. Matt Simpson

I saw my friend, ten years dead,
stuffed into a corner of the bookshop café
not looking up, stuffing himself with cake,
a pot of tea in front of him, brewing quietly.
Was he doing the crossword?
Or writing a poem, unable to stop himself
on one of his weekly trips to town
where he might buy a coveted CD
and browse poetry sections for the latest thing.
It took some willpower to stop myself
from going over, saying *Hello Matt,
long time no see. They told me you were dead.*
He was fine, slightly plumper, his white hair
as thick as ever. How long after they are gone
do the dead stop giving us false hope?

IX. WOMEN IN LIFE AND LITERATURE

I will not be silenced. I have things to say

Miranda Plans

Be not afeard; the isle is full of noises,
Sounds and sweet airs, that give delight, and hurt not.

The Tempest

My toys were sea glass, shells and pebbles.
In my cove by the rocks, I made patterns
with feathery bryopsis and flaky maerl.

This was the only home I remembered.
My other life at court was a storybook,
the boat we arrived in bore witness.

In my father's cave I was lulled and shushed
and the song of the sea was my nursemaid.
I learned to weave baskets and thread necklaces.

Caliban was my friend, and together we swam
in amethyst waters, listened to the island's spirits
for this place is full of sounds and sweet airs.

I grew up here, learned to catch and gut fish,
take out fulmar and guillemot with my bow,
harvest plants and nuts, cook over an open fire.

Now Father says we have to leave. He's told me
some long tale about how he was a Duke,
and set his sights on this prince for me to marry,

I don't see what it's got to do with me. And the prince
is all fancy talk and heavy sighs. Not like Caliban,
already a king, though sometimes he acts the fool.

Cal's scared of Father, ever since he caught us,
so I have to pretend to like this Ferdinand.
I'm just biding my time, castling my king.

Writing Broken-Hearted

Not just the wide moors and hard-bitten country
but Yorkshire mills, factory floors,
machinery and the fight for rights.

Not just romance but humour of curates
covering the town like snow on hills
waiting for Charlotte to write them.

Her own Mr Nicholls not so quarrelsome.
He relished her sharp portrayals,
knowing she didn't mean *him*.

While she wrote, her world fell apart:
Branwell, Emily, Anne all hacking blood,
succumbing to the illness they dreaded.

All she could do, to escape the grief, was write.
In the numb blankness of the house's silence,
the only sounds were her pen scritch-scratching,

relentless clock marking time, Father
alone with his books, softly breathing,
the fire, and wind soughing round the house.

Did her tears blot the pages, as she thought of
her sisters writing beside her no more,
their comradely appreciation of each other?

Or did she choke her tears in the writing
as Caroline and Shirley talk of poetry.
Cowper's hand did not tremble in writing the lines.

Maggie Tulliver Saved

I swam away from Eliot's pen.
She was writing my death because
her time had run out for my story.

She wrote of the world she knew
but my head bobbed up from the river
in a different time.

My waterlogged Victorian clothes
I sent back with the stream.
Who wants to wear such skirts?

They restrict and I will not be caged
nor coffined. I stride away
from the water's edge, into a future.

Call me Malala, call me Greta.
I will not be silenced. I have things to say
that will shake your world.

Nita's Knitted Wardrobe

Garments from the Yorkshire Fashion Archive

Nita wore only haute couture:
garments her mother knitted without patterns,
copying catwalk trends and fashion magazines,
peering at window displays with a sketchpad.

Anything Nita wanted: tailored suits
winter coats with astrakhan collars,
fitted dresses, smart jackets.
Always four ply, wool or cotton,
with zips and facings, lined just like the real thing.
Isora could mimic tweed, tartan,
brocade and linen, even houndstooth.

Her needles clicked like little engines,
clockworking the hours, each garment
finished in days, ticktocking regular rhythms
of purl and plain, cable and lace, inventiveness
solving every difficulty.

Her head was a library of stitches:
andaloo, parquet, bramble, butterfly, tree of life,
jack-in-the-pulpit, double lattice, woven stitch,
lucine, eye of the lynx, hearts, lily of the valley,
travelling vine, mermaid's mesh.

She wanted her daughter smart as better-off cousins,
whose father, unlike Nita's, hadn't run off to America.
All she'd brought from Russia in 1904 was her skill,
family tailoring embedded in her skull.

The night she died, Isora finished a flared dress,
couldn't leave until she'd sewn the seams. Nita
wouldn't wear any other clothes. Her mother's love
was caught in every fibre, keeping her safe.

A lifetime in Isora's designs:
Nita wore them in the care home,
where they felted in the washing machine,
shrunk to fit her skinny frame.

Her son Michael brought them in
didn't know if they were any use.

Cheshire Dig 2529

On the site of an ancient
twentieth century house
a haul of objects dusted clean.
Exhibit One: green and lilac spectacles
indicating the owner needed
corrective eye surgery.

Exhibit Two: shell button, once used
to fasten clothes. Note the traces
of a bird painting, which dates it
before such things became extinct.
This one is black with a yellow bill.
History suggests they were once common.

Note: we've found many bird bones
near dwellings of the 22nd century
indicating that in times of famine
they were a valuable food source.

The person who lived here
was not rich but owned
many items of personal adornment
such as Exhibits three, four and five,
a plain gold ring, silver earrings
set of beads made from fossilised amber.

From the many fragments of ancient text
and a few intact bound books
some printed and some handwritten
we think the owner may have been a scribe.

Unfortunately paper rots quite quickly
and ink soon degrades in damp.
That's all. The land can now be cleared.

Acknowledgements

MAGAZINES:

Bakings, BODY, Clear Poetry, Interlitq, Live Encounters, Magma, Marble, Orbis, Pennine Platform, Poetry Scotland, Sadie Girl Press (USA), *Southlight, Stand, Stride, The Black Light Engine Room, The Curlew, The High Window, The Interpreter's House, The Lake, The Wild Word.*

ANTHOLOGIES:

An Insubstantial Universe (Yaffle 2020), *Be Not Afraid: An Anthology in Appreciation of Seamus Heaney* (Lapwing 2018),) *Bonnie's Crew* (2018), *Crossings Over: Poetry from the Cheshire Prize for Literature 2016* (University of Chester Press 2017), *Humankind: Writing from the Cheshire Prize for Literature 2022* (Chester University Press 2023), *#MeToo* (Fairacre Press 2018), *Please Hear What I'm Not Saying* (Fly on the Wall Press 2018), *Shepton Mallet Snowdrop Festival Competition Anthology 2019, Sleeping in Frozen Quiet* (Indigo Dreams 2023), *Sweet Breast and Acid Tongue* (Like This Press 2013), *Tower of Babel* (with Rupert Loydell, Like This Press, 2013), *Witches, Warriors, Workers* (Culture Matters 2020), *Wolverhampton Literature Festival Competition Anthology 2018,* Beautiful Dragons Anthologies: *Heavenly Bodies* (2014), *The Bee's Breakfast,* (2017), *Noble Dissent,* (2017), *Watch the Birdie* (2018), *Well, Dam!* (2019), *Lighting Out* (2021).

OTHER:

'Mother of Pearl' won first prize in the Crewe and District Writers Circle Competition (2018).

'Light and Moths' featured in single poem films for National Poetry Day 2015 created by Poetry Ambassador Liz Brownlee.

'Plank Figurine' was commissioned by Eleanor Livingstone, for StAnza 2019, based on an artefact held at The Museum of St Andrews. It was shown on the media screens and used in a set of postcards.

'Patching the Cashmere' appeared on Fife Contemporary in a feature called 'Resolve to Make It New', in collaboration with StAnza 2022.

'Writing in the Body' is my side of a conversation in poetry with Aaron Kent (*Poetic Interview*s Broken Sleep Books 2019).